T0012301

Being in Government

So You Want to Be
SUPREME COURT JUSTICE

by Dr. Artika R. Tyner

Consultant:
Fred Slocum,
Associate Professor of Political Science,
Minnesota State University, Mankato

CAPSTONE PRESS
a capstone imprint

Fact Finders Books are published by Capstone Press
1710 Roe Crest Drive, North Mankato, Minnesota 56003
www.mycapstone.com

Library of Congress Cataloging-in-Publication Data
Names: Tyner, Artika R., author.
Title: So you want to be a Supreme Court justice / by Artika R. Tyner.
Description: North Mankato, Minnesota : Capstone Press, 2019. | Series: Being
    in Government
Identifiers: LCCN 2019004862 | ISBN 9781543571974 (hardcover) | ISBN
    9781543575279 (paperback) | ISBN 9781543572018 (ebook pdf)
Subjects: LCSH: United States. Supreme Court—Officials and
    employees—Selection and appointment—Juvenile literature. |
    Judges—Selection and appointment—United States—Juvenile literature.
Classification: LCC KF8742 .T96 2019 | DDC 347.73/2634023—dc23
LC record available at https://lccn.loc.gov/2019004862

Editorial Credits
Mari Bolte, editor; Jennifer Bergstrom, designer;
Jo Miller, media researcher; Laura Manthe, production specialist

Photo Credits
AP Images, 10; Capstone Studio: Karon Dubke, Cover; Newscom: Pool via CNP/Kevin
Dietsch, 17, Reuters/Kevin Lamarque, 13, 27, US Supreme Court/Steve Petteway, 5, ZUMA
Press/Michael Evans, 21, ZUMA Press/US Senate, 29; Shutterstock: dikbraziy, 20, fstockfoto,
19, Jer123, 7, Rob Crandall, 14, stock_photo_world, 18; Wikimedia: Collection of the
Supreme Court of the United States, Photographer: Steve Petteway, 23, 24, 25, United States
Government, 8

Design Elements
Capstone; Shutterstock: hchjjl, MSSA, primiaou, Rebellion Works, simbos

Printed in the United States of America.
PA70

TABLE OF CONTENTS

WANTED:
PROBLEM SOLVER AND TOP LAWYER

Do you work well with others? Do you have a passion for problem-solving? Do you want to make decisions that shape the entire country? Do you want a job for life? Then this powerful and important position may be for you!

Unlike other seats in government, there are no written requirements to become a Supreme Court justice. You do not have to be a specific age, though most justices are in their 50s or older. You also do not have to be born or live anywhere special.

Although there is technically no requirement for it, a background in law is essential. The Supreme Court is the highest court in the United States. Every justice who has ever served on the Court has been a lawyer.

FACT: As of 2018 all the sitting justices attended either Harvard or Yale Law School.

Chief Justice John G. Roberts (right) swears in justice Elena Kagan to the Supreme Court in 2010.

JOBS AND PAYDAYS

In 2018 an associate justice's salary was $255,300 a year. All the Supreme Court justices are associates, except for the chief justice. The chief justice leads the Supreme Court during public hearings and private conferences. He or she is chairperson of the court. The chief justice's salary was $267,000. Justices usually get raises every year.

Chapter 2

FOLLOWING THE LAW

The United States Supreme Court is part of the judicial branch of government. Congress, which is made up of the House of Representatives and the Senate, is part of the legislative branch. This branch considers and passes laws. The president is part of the executive branch. He or she approves or denies those laws. Then the judicial branch ensures those laws are followed. Sometimes the courts hear complaints or suggest changes about those laws.

Courts hear complaints and settle disputes. They listen to both sides to decide what really happened. In criminal cases, they decide if someone committed a crime. Then they decide whether and how that person should be punished.

The United States has 94 district courts, 13 appeals courts, and one Supreme Court.

Civil cases usually involve private complaints between people or organizations. For example, a landlord might take tenants to civil court for not paying their rent. The judge or jury decides who is responsible for wrongdoing. Usually the wrongdoer is ordered to pay money.

Criminal cases involve the government claiming a person or group has broken the law. Kidnapping and murder trials are two examples of criminal cases. A jury decides if someone is guilty or not guilty. Prison is a common punishment for the guilty.

The federal court system has three levels—district courts, appeals courts, and the Supreme Court. The lowest level is district court. Most court cases start here. District courts handle both civil and criminal trials. Witnesses are heard. A jury, or sometimes a judge, makes a decision based on evidence heard from the witnesses.

Commonly, once a district court gives a ruling, the case is over. However, those on the losing side can appeal if they believe the district court was unfair, the judge applied the wrong law, or the law was applied incorrectly. The appeals courts—more formally known as "circuit courts of appeals"—have to agree to hear a case.

In the appeals court, three judges hear arguments on why the district court ruling should be overturned or upheld. Lawyers on both sides make their arguments and answer any questions the judges may have. The judges do not hear witnesses, and no new evidence can be introduced. District courts are concerned with learning the facts of a case, but appeals courts rule based on legal procedure.

There are 11 circuit courts of appeals across the country. Each is responsible for a different region.

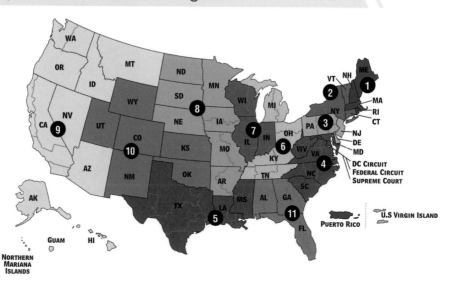

A FAMOUS APPEAL:
GLIK V. CUNNIFFE

In 2011 lawyer Simon Glik recorded police officers making a violent arrest at a park in Boston, Massachusetts. The officers noticed and arrested Glik. He was charged with **wiretapping**, disturbing the peace, and aiding the escape of a prisoner. The district court ruled in his favor, and the charges were dropped.

However, afterward Glik filed a civil suit against the city of Boston, saying his arrest violated his **constitutional** rights. The First Circuit Court of Appeals ruled that Glik's rights were violated and that he had the right to record the police. The city of Boston agreed that Glik's arrest was wrong.

The D.C. Circuit Court of Appeals only takes cases in the District of Columbia. These cases usually relate to the federal government or its agencies. The Federal Circuit Court of Appeals handles specialized cases involving international trade, copyrights, patents, and trademarks.

constitutional—having to do with an important set of rules or laws, as for a nation

wiretap—to place a device on a telephone line that allows conversations to be heard secretly

Thurgood Marshall (center) was one of the lawyers involved with *Brown v. Board of Education*. He became a Supreme Court justice in 1967.

The Supreme Court is the highest level court in the United States. It reviews cases from both state and federal courts. Every year the Supreme Court receives between 8,000 and 10,000 requests, called writs of certiorari. The justices meet to choose their cases based on those writs. Four of the nine justices must grant certiorari, or agree to hear the case. If they do not agree, certiorari is denied, and the appeals court decision becomes final. In all, the Supreme Court hears only 1 percent of the total submitted cases.

HOW MANY?

The Supreme Court was created by Congress in 1789. Originally, there were six justices.

The number of justices increased and decreased several times after that. Since 1869 the Supreme Court has been made up of nine justices—one chief justice and eight associate justices.

Some cases involve conflicting laws across the country. In *Brown v. Board of Education of Topeka* in 1954, the Supreme Court decided that **segregation** in public schools was **unconstitutional**. This eventually led to school **integration** across the United States. The ruling also overturned the decision made in *Plessy v. Ferguson* in 1896. In this case, the Supreme Court had ruled that segregation by law in public places did not violate equal rights.

integration—the practice of including people of all races in schools and other public places

segregation—the practice of keeping groups of people apart, especially based on race

unconstitutional—not in agreement with the Constitution

Chapter 3

BECOMING A JUSTICE

Ready to get the job done? There are a lot of steps involved!

Supreme Court justices do not run for office. They are not elected or re-elected. They do not have term limits. They serve for life or until they choose to retire. And there are only nine seats. So how do you become a justice?

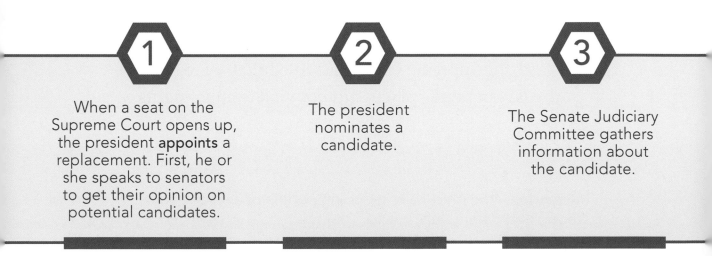

1

When a seat on the Supreme Court opens up, the president **appoints** a replacement. First, he or she speaks to senators to get their opinion on potential candidates.

2

The president nominates a candidate.

3

The Senate Judiciary Committee gathers information about the candidate.

The Senate Judiciary Committee debated Samuel Alito Jr.'s nomination. He was nominated in 2005 and confirmed in 2006.

4

The candidate answers a questionnaire of personal information.

5

The American Bar Association, a neutral organization of lawyers and law students, checks the candidate's professional work and gives it a rating.

appoint—to choose someone for a job

If a candidate is confirmed, he or she is sworn in. Then the new justice takes two oaths: The Constitutional Oath and the Judicial Oath. Clarence Thomas took his oaths in 1991.

6

The candidate meets with senators in one-on-one meetings.

7

The Federal Bureau of Investigation (FBI) investigates the nominee and shares its findings with the Senate Judiciary Committee.

8

The Senate Judiciary Committee invites the candidate to a public hearing, which usually lasts four to five days.

ASKING THE QUESTIONS

At the Senate Judiciary Committee hearing, the candidate must answer questions about his or her qualifications, beliefs, the Constitution, past court cases, and other questions relating to the law.

The hearings were not always televised. Sandra Day O'Connor's hearing was the first, in 1981. Before, many senators did not bother to attend hearings. Once they were televised, though, nearly every senator showed up. In 2018 more than 20 million people across the country watched Brett Kavanaugh's hearing.

FACT: Supreme Court justices serve an average of 17 years. Justice William O. Douglas served for 36 years, 7 months, and 8 days. Chief Justice John Rutledge served in a temporary position for just 5 months and 14 days.

9

The Senate Judiciary Committee meets to determine if it can recommend the candidate to the rest of the Senate.

10

If the candidate is recommended, the Senate discusses and debates the nomination. Then senators vote on whether or not to confirm the candidate.

Chapter 4

AT WORK

Supreme Court justices work at the United States Supreme Court Building in Washington, D.C. The main entrance faces the United States Capitol. A courtyard out front shows off two fountains. Large statues sit at the base of the steps into the building. The steps lead to huge bronze doors that weigh 6.5 tons (5.9 metric tons) each.

The building has four levels. The ground floor contains offices, information for visitors, and police headquarters.

Walking up the courtyard stairs leads to the first floor and into the Great Hall. There you can view busts of the former chief justices. Then head down the hall to the Court Chamber. This is the primary room where justices work.

The rest of the first floor has offices for justices, law clerks, secretaries, and other officials. There are also meeting rooms, a lounge, and a Robing Room.

The official Supreme Court photo, November 2018. Front row, from left: Stephen Breyer, Clarence Thomas, Chief Justice John G. Roberts, Ruth Bader Ginsburg, and Samuel Alito Jr. Back row: Neil Gorsuch, Sonia Sotomayor, Elena Kagan, and Brett M. Kavanaugh.

THE ROBING ROOM

Federal and state judges across the United States wear long, black robes while in court. The robes symbolize that all judges share the common responsibility of upholding the laws and the Constitution.

Before Supreme Court justices hear arguments, they dress in the Robing Room. Attendants help them fasten their robes. Then the justices all shake hands before walking into the courtroom.

The second floor of the Supreme Court Building contains more offices. There is also a reading room and a dining room for the justices. The third floor is a huge library with more than 500,000 books.

Visitors to the Supreme Court Building can tour the first and ground floors. They can also sit in the courtroom during oral arguments.

The Supreme Court Building is open to the public between 9 a.m. and 4:30 p.m. on weekdays.

The Supreme Court Building has been home to the justices since 1935.

WHERE ARE WE MEETING?

The first justices met in New York City; Philadelphia; and then in the District of Columbia. In D.C. they used space in the Capitol Building. Finally, former president and sitting Chief Justice William Howard Taft led the efforts to build the Supreme Court Building in 1929. Construction began in 1932 and was completed in 1935.

The Supreme Court begins a new term on the first Monday of October. The justices spend part of that time "sitting," during which time they hear cases and deliver opinions. On half the Mondays, Tuesdays, and Wednesdays of the month, they hear two cases a day. Members of the public can come hear the cases.

The justices have already decided in advance which cases to hear. The Court looks over each case's history beforehand in documents called briefs. At the hearings, attorneys on each side are given 30 minutes to speak.

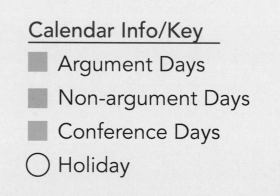

DIFFERENT VOICES

A strong team brings together different life experiences. They reflect the diversity of the United States. Here are some notable firsts on the Supreme Court:

Louis B. Brandeis
(1916–1939)
first Jewish justice

Thurgood Marshall
(1967–1991)
first African American justice

Sandra Day O'Connor
(1981–2006)
first female justice

Sonia Sotomayor
(2009–present)
first Hispanic justice

Sandra Day O'Connor was nominated by President Ronald Reagan and confirmed unanimously by the Senate.

However, of the 114 justices, only four have been women—Sandra Day O'Connor, Ruth Bader Ginsburg (1993–present), Sonia Sotomayor, and Elena Kagan (2010–present). Thurgood Marshall, Sonia Sotomayor, and Clarence Thomas (1991–present) have been the only justices of color. There have been no American Indian or Asian American justices. There also has never been a Muslim justice. There's a long way to go!

21

On Fridays the justices meet privately to discuss the arguments they have heard in Court. Then they vote on each case. There are nine justices to ensure that a vote never ends in a tie. If at least five justices agree, that is the majority opinion.

A FAMOUS DISSENT

Dred Scott was an enslaved person who lived with his owner in a free territory for many years. He was married and had a child in free territory. When he tried to buy his family's freedom, his owner refused. Scott sued, claiming that he had been free the minute he passed into a place that outlawed slavery.

On March 6, 1857, the Supreme Court ruled on *Dred Scott v. Sandford*. By a 7–2 decision, Chief Justice Roger Taney announced that black people in the United States could not sue because they were not citizens.

Justice Benjamin R. Curtis dissented. He believed that the Constitution was clear when it said, "All men are created equal." Scott was a man and a citizen. Justice John McLean agreed. "Being born under our Constitution and laws, no naturalization is required . . . to make him a citizen," he wrote.

The *Dred Scott* decision was overturned when the 13th, 14th, and 15th **amendments** were passed. The 13th ended slavery. The 14th defined citizenship and what protections citizens are given. The 15th gave citizens the right to vote, regardless of race, color, or previous enslavement.

Afterward, justices write opinions. The chief justice decides who will write the majority opinion. The majority opinion explains the Court's decision and the reasoning behind it. Sometimes justices write a concurring opinion, in which they agree with the majority side but disagree with the reasoning the majority uses. Other justices may write **dissenting** opinions about why they disagree with the majority vote.

Justice Ruth Bader Ginsburg is known for her dissents. She is also known for the white collars, called jabots, that she wears with her robes. She has a special jabot for days she writes dissents.

amendment—a change made to a law or a legal document

dissent—to disagree with the opinion of others

The time the Supreme Court is not hearing cases is called recess. While in recess, the justices write opinions on cases they have heard, research upcoming cases, and decide whether to hear potential future cases. The justices alternate sitting in court and being in recess every two weeks through April. They spend May and June looking over possible future cases and announcing opinions. Then they break for a longer recess in the summer. They continue to review potential new cases. They also use this time to teach, write, or travel.

Do you like to be in charge? The Supreme Court's leader is the chief justice. The president nominates the chief justice. Then the Senate votes on whether or not to confirm the choice. Sometimes the chief justice has served as an associate justice, but not always. The chief justice holds that position until he or she dies, retires, or resigns from the court.

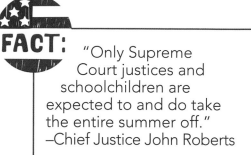

FACT: "Only Supreme Court justices and schoolchildren are expected to and do take the entire summer off." —Chief Justice John Roberts

John Roberts
(1955–   )

WORK AND PLAY

Although justices spend a lot of time working, they also have fun. Some, like Anthony Kennedy or John Roberts, have spent their summer recess teaching or visiting overseas. Clarence Thomas and his wife use the summer to drive cross-country in a motor home. Others write books about their lives or about judicial matters. Ruth Bader Ginsburg wrote a book about her workout routine.

Sonia Sotomayor has written a memoir, as well as two books for children, about her life.

During **inaugurations**, the chief justice administers the oath of office to the president and vice president. The chief justice is also the leader of the Judicial Conference of the United States, an organization of 26 federal judges. They study how different courts work around the country and discuss how they can be improved.

inauguration—formal ceremony to swear a person into political office

Chapter 5

WHAT NOW?

Since many justices are older when they are appointed, and the appointment is for life, sometimes they have served until their deaths. Between 1876 and 1900, 38 of 57 justices did just that. But because people today live longer, that is a much rarer occurrence. Between 1955 and 2005 no sitting justices died while in office.

But what happens when they take off the robe?

After leaving the Supreme Court, they can still serve on lower federal courts. Some take what's known as senior status. Their age plus their years of court service must total 80 to qualify—for example, a 65-year-old judge would need 15 years of experience. They must do the same work as an active judge for at least three months of the year. Others simply serve on lower courts as circuit or district judges.

Former justice Sandra Day O'Connor has served on appeals courts around the nation since her retirement in 2006.

 FACT: Justices have access to health insurance benefits and a pension in retirement. They can also earn extra money by writing books or teaching classes.

THE ROAD TO THE COURT

Each justice has traveled a unique path to reach his or her position in the highest court in the United States. But a background in law is key to getting there!

It's never too early to start. Find a copy of the Constitution and get familiar with its words. Study the amendments and research what led to their creation. How has each amendment changed the way we live in the United States?

Follow current events. Think about how each event falls within the law. Take a moment to consider that there may be another side to the story. Read about the event from various news sources. Then make your own decision.

Civil rights leader and congressman John Lewis (center) holding up a copy of the Constitution in March 2016. He was urging the Senate to select a Supreme Court nominee.

As you get older, talk to a guidance counselor about your options. Consider the time it takes to become a lawyer, and consider the cost (becoming a lawyer requires a college degree, plus three years of law school, then passing the bar exam in your state). Look into scholarships and grants. Visit law offices and ask the lawyers questions about what they do. They may have some good advice to give the next Supreme Court justice!

GLOSSARY

amendment (uh-MEND-muhnt)—a change made to a law or a legal document

appoint (uh-POINT)—to choose someone for a job

constitutional (kahn-stuh-TOO-shuh-nuhl)—having to do with an important set of rules or laws, as for a nation

dissent (di-SENT)—to disagree with the opinion of others

executive branch (ig-ZE-kyuh-tiv BRANCH)—the part of government that makes sure laws are obeyed

inauguration (in-AW-gyuh-ray-shuhn)—formal ceremony to swear a person into political office

integration (in-tuh-GRAY-shuhn)—the practice of including people of all races in schools and other public places

judicial branch (joo-DISH-uhl BRANCH)—the part of government that explains laws

legislative branch (LEJ-iss-lay-tiv BRANCH)—the part of government that passes bills that become laws

segregation (seg-ruh-GAY-shuhn)—the practice of keeping groups of people apart, especially based on race

unconstitutional (un-kon-stuh-TOO-shuhn-uhl)—not in agreement with the Constitution

wiretap (WIRE-tap)—to place a device on a telephone line that allows conversations to be heard secretly; used to get information

READ MORE

Micklos Jr., John. *Ruth Bader Ginsburg: Get to Know the Justice Who Speaks Her Mind*. North Mankato, MN: Capstone Press, 2019.

Sotomayor, Sonia. *The Beloved World of Sonia Sotomayor*. New York: Delacorte Books for Young Readers, 2018.

Stoltman, Joan. *20 Fun Facts About the Supreme Court*. New York: Gareth Stevens Publishing, 2018.

INTERNET SITES

Current U.S. Supreme Court Justices
https://www.law.cornell.edu/supct/justices/fullcourt.html

SCOTUSblog
https://www.scotusblog.com/

Supreme Court of the United States
https://www.supremecourt.gov/

CRITICAL THINKING QUESTIONS

1. Justices must go through a long hearing process before they are confirmed. Why do you think that is? Watch a confirmation online. Do you think the senators asked the right questions? What kind of questions would you ask?
2. Name the three branches of government. Then explain what each branch does, and how they work together.
3. Since the Constitution was written in 1787, there have been 27 amendments. Read through each amendment. Choose one. Explain why you think it was written. Do you agree or disagree with the amendment?

INDEX